Date: 9/29/15

J BIO DISNEY
Hansen, Grace,
Walt Disney : animator & founder

Walt Disney

Animator & Founder

by Grace Hansen

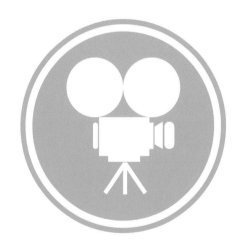

ABDO
HISTORY MAKER BIOGRAPHIES
Kids

abdopublishing.com

Published by Abdo Kids, a division of ABDO, PO Box 398166, Minneapolis, Minnesota 55439.

Copyright © 2015 by Abdo Consulting Group, Inc. International copyrights reserved in all countries. No part of this book may be reproduced in any form without written permission from the publisher.

Printed in the United States of America, North Mankato, Minnesota.

102014

012015

 THIS BOOK CONTAINS RECYCLED MATERIALS

Photo Credits: AP Images, Corbis, Getty Images, Glow Images, iStock, Shutterstock, © Recuerdos de Pandora / CC-SA-2.0 p.5

Production Contributors: Teddy Borth, Jennie Forsberg, Grace Hansen

Design Contributors: Laura Rask, Dorothy Toth

Library of Congress Control Number: 2014943716

Cataloging-in-Publication Data

Hansen, Grace.

 Walt Disney: animator & founder / Grace Hansen.

  p. cm. -- (History maker biographies)

Includes index.

ISBN 978-1-62970-706-8

1. Disney, Walt, 1901-1966--Juvenile literature. 2. Animators --United States--Biography--Juvenile literature. 1. Title.

791.43/092--dc23

[B]

2014943716

Table of Contents

Early Life

Walter Elias Disney was born on December 5, 1901. He was born in Chicago, Illinois.

Illinois

As a boy, Walt loved to draw. He sold his art to family and friends. He took drawing classes in school.

7

In 1919, Walt moved to Missouri.
He worked at the Kansas City
Film Ad Company. There he
learned about **animation**.

8

To Hollywood!

In 1923, Walt moved to Hollywood, California. His brother Roy joined him. They started Disney Bros. Studio.

Mickey Mouse

By 1928 the studio had grown. Walt had created Mickey Mouse. He **featured** Mickey in **silent cartoons**.

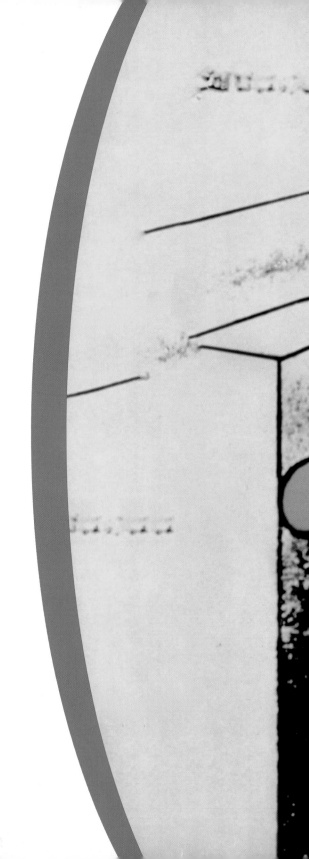

13

The cartoons did not do well.

So, Walt added sound.

He voiced Mickey Mouse

in *Steamboat Willie*.

It was very **popular**.

15

Animated Films

In 1937, Walt **released** his first film. It was called *Snow White and the Seven Dwarfs*. By 1964 Walt had made more than 18 films!

Legacy

Walt's last big success

was *Mary Poppins*. This

film **released** in 1964.

In 1966, Walt passed away.

19

Walt's greatest dream would come true. His brother made sure of it. Walt Disney World opened in 1971.

21

Timeline

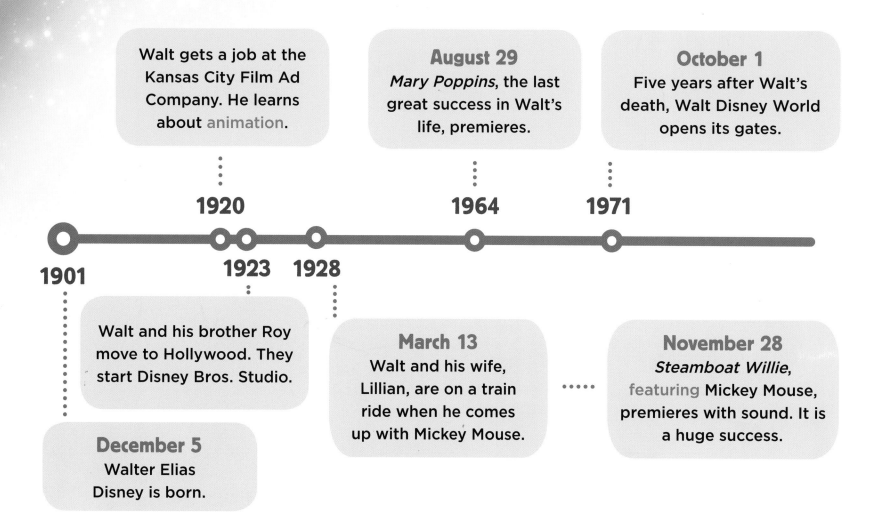

Walt gets a job at the Kansas City Film Ad Company. He learns about animation.

August 29
Mary Poppins, the last great success in Walt's life, premieres.

October 1
Five years after Walt's death, Walt Disney World opens its gates.

1920

1964

1971

1901

1923

1928

Walt and his brother Roy move to Hollywood. They start Disney Bros. Studio.

March 13
Walt and his wife, Lillian, are on a train ride when he comes up with Mickey Mouse.

November 28
Steamboat Willie, featuring Mickey Mouse, premieres with sound. It is a huge success.

December 5
Walter Elias Disney is born.

Glossary

animation – the process of giving movement to drawings.

release – make available for public viewing.

featured – presented as a special or main attraction.

silent cartoons – a cartoon without any words or sound.

popular – liked or enjoyed by many people.

Index

abdokids.com